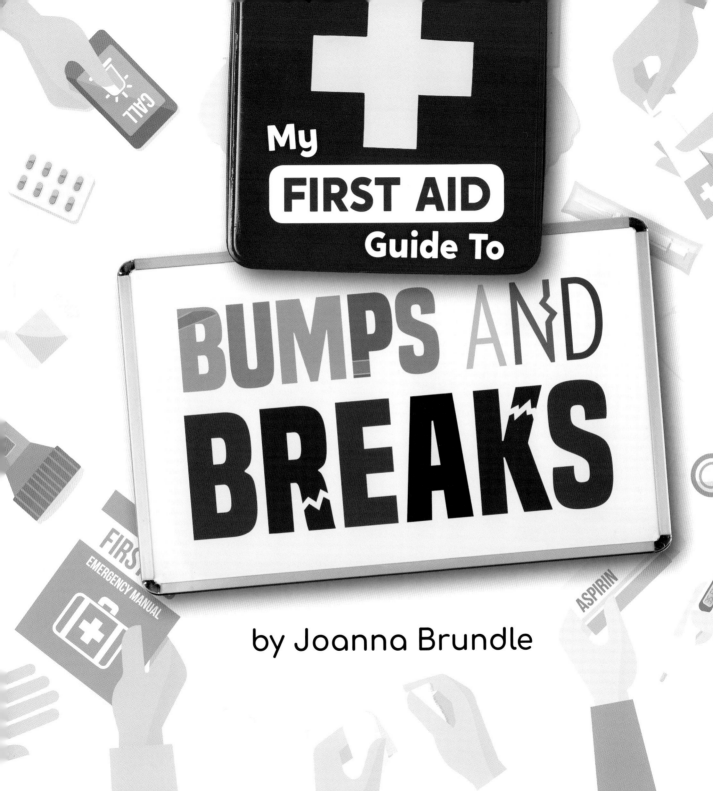

My
FIRST AID
Guide To

BUMPS AND
BREAKS

by Joanna Brundle

BookLife
PUBLISHING

©2019
BookLife Publishing Ltd.
King's Lynn
Norfolk PE30 4LS

All rights reserved.
Printed in Malaysia.

A catalogue record for this
book is available from the
British Library.

ISBN: 978-1-78637-832-3

Written by:
Joanna Brundle

Edited by:
William Anthony

Designed by:
Laura Gatie

*All facts, statistics, web
addresses and URLs in this
book were verified as valid
and accurate at time of writing.
No responsibility for any
changes to external websites
or references can be accepted
by either the author or
publisher.*

Photocredits

CONTENTS

Words that look like <u>this</u> can be found in the glossary on page 24.

WHAT IS FIRST AID?

First aid is help that is given to someone straight after they have hurt themselves, had an accident or become sick. First aid can be given by anyone, including you.

This girl is being helped by her friend.

Someone who is hurt is called a casualty.

Learning simple first aid is important. You will learn how to help someone who is hurt or what to do in a <u>medical emergency</u>. First aid lessons could even help you to save someone's life.

CALLING AN AMBULANCE

Emergency Ambulance

Listen and watch out for the ambulance.

Call an ambulance by dialling the emergency number in your country. You can also call 112 on any mobile phone in most countries around the world. Tell the person who answers that you need an ambulance and where you are.

6

While you are waiting, talk to the injured person and let them know that help is coming. Try not to move them as this could make their injury worse. Try and get help from an adult if you can.

Use a blanket, your coat or your jumper to keep the person warm.

BUMPS AND BRUISES

When someone bumps themselves, they may get a bruise. Bruises are caused by bleeding under the <u>surface</u> of the skin. Treat a bruise by holding something cold over the area.

Bruises can be blue, black or dark red.

You can use a bag of frozen vegetables to make an <u>ice pack</u>. Wrap the bag in a cloth first. A cold flannel works well too. Use a cushion to lift up the bruised part.

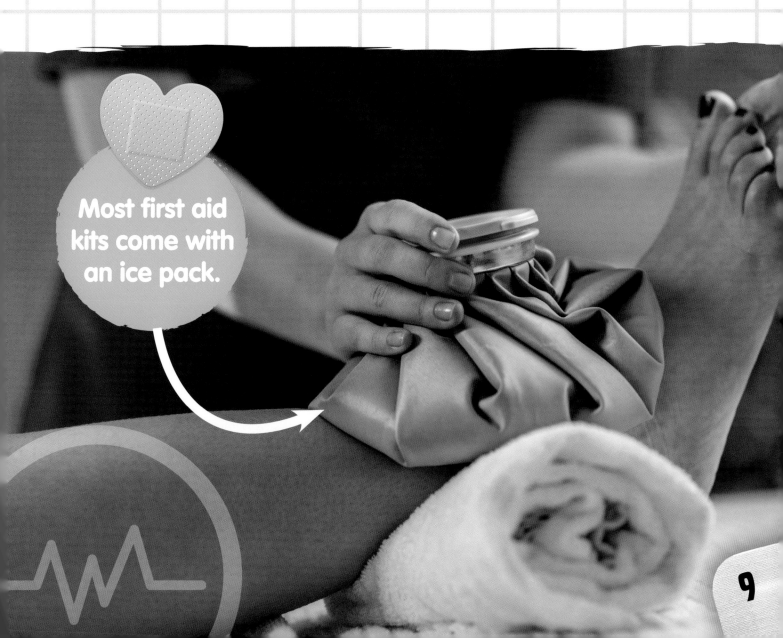

Most first aid kits come with an ice pack.

9

SPRAINS AND STRAINS

Sprains and strains are injuries to <u>soft tissue</u> around ankles, wrists and other joints. They cause pain, <u>swelling</u> and bruising, and they make it hard for someone to move. To treat sprains and strains, remember RICE.

Falling when you are skateboarding could cause a sprain.

REST

Lay or sit the person down, with the hurt part of the body raised.

ICE

Hold an ice pack on the area.

COMPRESS

Tie a support bandage around the area.

ELEVATE

Lift and support the area that is hurt by using something soft, such as cushions.

HEAD INJURIES

A bump to the head can cause a <u>graze</u> and a headache. A lump might appear because of bleeding under the skin. Hold something cold on the injured area and make sure the person rests.

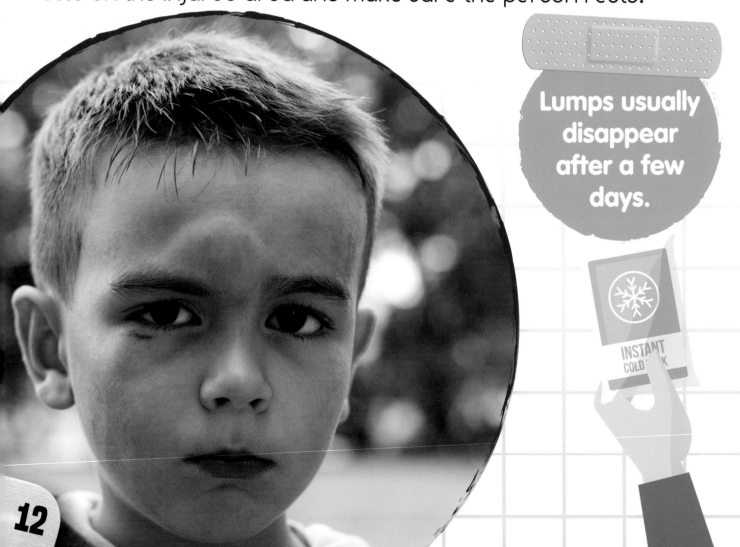

Lumps usually disappear after a few days.

INSTANT COLD PACK

Headguards are worn in some sports to try to stop head injuries.

Concussion is an injury to the brain caused by getting bumped on the head. It can cause a bad headache, <u>vomiting</u> and sleepiness. If this happens, or if the person was knocked <u>unconscious</u>, call an ambulance.

13

THE AVPU SCALE

People act in different ways after a bump on the head, depending on how bad their injury is. You can use the AVPU scale to find out how <u>alert</u> someone is after a head injury.

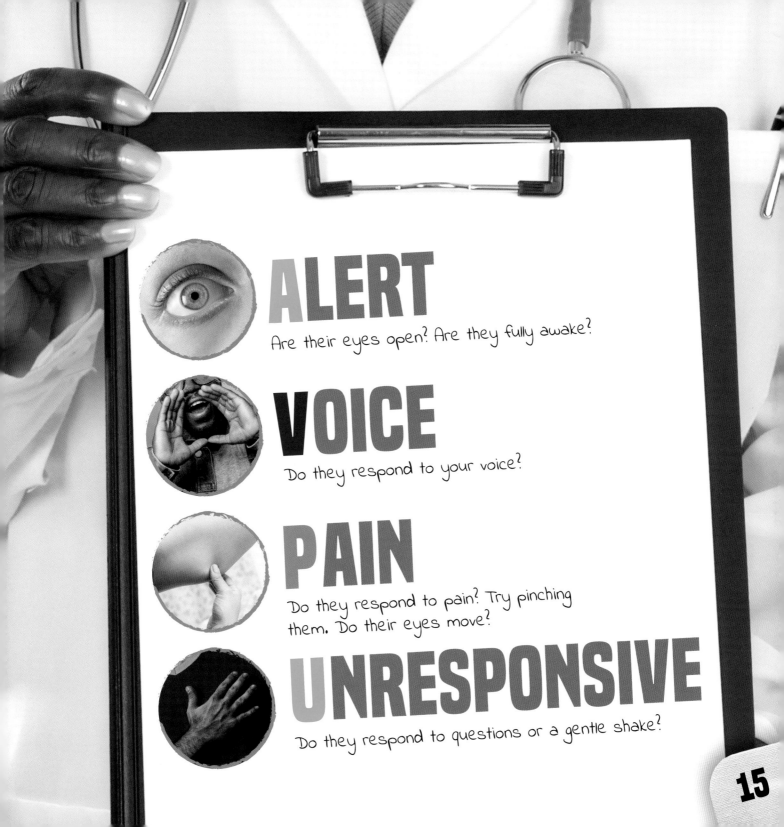

ALERT
Are their eyes open? Are they fully awake?

VOICE
Do they respond to your voice?

PAIN
Do they respond to pain? Try pinching them. Do their eyes move?

UNRESPONSIVE
Do they respond to questions or a gentle shake?

15

BREAKS

A break or crack in a bone is called a fracture. If the broken bone is still under the skin, it is a closed fracture. If the broken bone comes through the skin, it is an open fracture.

Signs of a break include bruising, swelling and difficulty moving.

Greenstick fractures are often caused by a fall.

Bones that are still growing are soft. Instead of breaking in two, only part of the bone cracks and the rest bends. Breaks like this are called greenstick fractures.

HELPING SOMEONE WITH A BREAK +

For an open fracture, cover the wound with a clean <u>dressing</u>. A first aid kit will have these. Press around the wound to stop any bleeding. Support the injured part to stop it from moving.

If you don't have a dressing, use a clean cloth or piece of clothing.

18

The broken part can be tied to an uninjured part to stop it from moving. For example, you can use bandages to tie a broken leg to the other leg or a broken finger to the next finger.

SHOCK

Shock happens when there is not enough blood flowing round the body. A bump or break can cause shock. Signs of shock include a pale face, cold skin, dizziness and fast breathing.

Shock can be serious. Learning to treat shock could save someone's life.

First, call an ambulance.
Then, lay the person down
with their legs higher than their
head, but don't move an injured
leg. Loosen any tight clothing
and use a coat or blanket to
keep them warm.

Raising the legs sends blood back to the brain.

21

THINGS TO REMEMBER

Learn the emergency numbers in case there is an emergency.

Learn your home address and postcode. If someone at home is poorly, you can say where an ambulance should be sent.

Before helping anyone, check you are safe. Move away and call for help if you spot any dangers, such as sharp objects or a spillage.

23

GLOSSARY

alert	able to think clearly and notice things
dressing	a piece of material used to cover and protect a wound
graze	a small wound caused by the skin scraping against something
ice pack	a bag filled with frozen things, or an item found in a first aid kit that gets very cold when it is squeezed or hit
medical emergency	a situation in which someone needs help from a medical professional straight away
soft tissue	soft parts of the body, such as muscles
surface	the outside layer of something
swelling	an area on someone's body that is larger than normal because of an injury
unconscious	not being awake or aware of what is happening
vomiting	being sick

INDEX